Ants

Melissa Stewart

NATIONAL GEOGRAPHIC
Washington, D.C.

For Claire, who sometimes seems to have
ants in her pants.— Melissa

Library of Congress Cataloging-in-Publication Data

Stewart, Melissa.
Ants! / by Melissa Stewart.
p. cm.
ISBN 978-1-4263-0609-9 (library binding : alk. paper) -- ISBN 978-1-4263-0608-2 (trade pbk. : alk.
paper)
1. Ants--Juvenile literature. I. Title.
QL568.F7S82 2010
595.79'6--dc22
2009035188

Cover: © George B. Diebold/ Corbis; 1, 6-7, 28 (inset), 30 (inset): © Shutterstock; 2: © Jason Edwards/ National Geographic/ Getty
Images; 4-5, 26: © Christian Ziegler/ Minden Pictures/ National Geographic Stock; 8, 16 (inset), 16-17, 22-23 (bottom), 23, 24 (inset),
32 (top, left), 32 (top, right), 32 (bottom, right): © Mark Moffett/ Minden Pictures; 9, 10: © iStockphoto; 10 (inset): © Robert Sisson/
National Geographic Stock; 11: © De Agostini Picture Library/ Getty Images; 12 (inset): © Satoshi Kuribayashi/ Minden Pictures; 13:
© Michael & Patricia Fogden/ Corbis; 14: © Dong Lin, California Academy of Sciences; 18, 32 (bottom, left): © Mark Moffett/ Minden
Pictures/ National Geographic Stock; 19: © Koshy Johnson/ OSF/ Photolibrary; 20-21: © Meul/ ARCO/ Nature Picture Library; 21 (inset):
© George Grall/ National Geographic/ Getty Images; 22: © Ajay Narendra, Australian National University, Canberra; 22-23 (top): ©
Carlo Bavagnoli/ Time Life Pictures/ Getty Images; 24 (background): © Piotr Naskrecki/ Minden Pictures; 25: © Visuals Unlimited/
Corbis; 26 (inset): © Piotr Naskrecki/ Minden Pictures/ National Geographic Stock; 28: © Clive Varlack; © John La Gette/ Alamy.

Printed in the United States of America
13/WOR/6

Table of Contents

Ants All Around

Do you know how many ants live in the world?

More than
10,000,000,000,000,000.
That's a lot of ants!

Ants live in fields and forests. They live under sidewalks too.

Ants are everywhere!

How do you say
10,000,000,000,000,000?
It's 10 quadrillion!
You say it like this:
kwa drill yun.

An ant is an active insect.

Its tiny waist helps it bend and wriggle through tunnels.

Its six strong legs creep and crawl.

Its two large eyes see the world.

Its super tough jaws munch and crunch.

Its long feelers touch and tap.

Wood Ant

Ants at Home

Army Ant Colony

One ant. Two ants.
Three ants. Four.
See one ant, and you'll
see lots more.

Ants live in large groups.
A group of ants is called
a colony.

WORD BITES

COLONY: A group of
ants that lives together.
Some colonies have
millions of ants.

An ant colony lives in a nest.
Most ants build nests underground.
An ant nest is full of tunnels.
Each tunnel leads to a little room.

Bulldog Ant
inside a tunnel

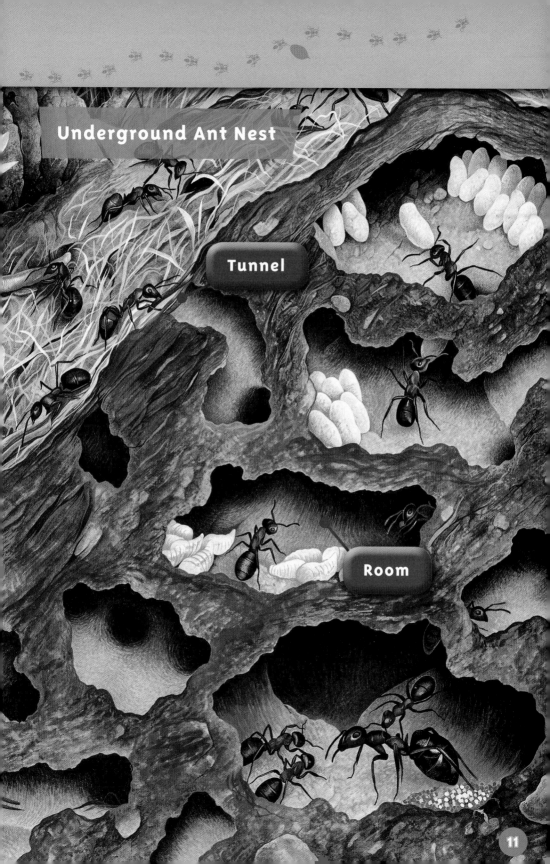

Underground Ant Nest

Tunnel

Room

Guinea Ant
nest in a tree

Some ants do not
live underground.

They live…
…inside hollow thorns.
…between rocks.
…in rotting trees.
…in nests made of leaves.

Weaver Ants

The Ant Man

Brian Fisher is a scientist. He looks for new kinds of ants. Some people call him **"The Ant Man."**

Dr. Fisher has found more than 800 new kinds of ants.

He can't wait to find even more!

An Ant's Life

Queen

Ant taking care of pupae

The queen is the biggest ant in a colony. She lays eggs all day long.

When the eggs hatch, little larvae wriggle out. They look like worms.

Aztec Ants

Egg

WORD BITES

LARVAE: The second stage in the life of many insects. Larvae spend most of their time eating and growing.

PUPAE: The third stage in the life of many insects. Some ant pupae are surrounded by a cocoon.

They eat and eat and eat.

Larvae turn into pupae. Pupae do not move. Pupae do not eat. After a few weeks, they turn into adult ants.

17

Worker Ants

Most of the ants in a colony are workers. All worker ants are female.

Inside the Nest

Some worker ants dig new tunnels. Others take care of eggs, larvae, and pupae.

Bulldog Ant

Larvae

Weaver Ants

Worker Ants

Many ants eat other insects.

Outside the Nest

Some worker ants collect food.

Others guard the nest.

Ants with Wings

Garden Ant

Winged Carpenter Ants

A few ants in the colony have wings.
Some are females. Some are males.

Ants with wings fly out of the nest.
They start new colonies.

Superhero Ants

Aqua Ant

Aqua Ant lives in Australia. She can swim, dive, and even live underwater.

Mama Marvel

Mama Marvel is an African driver ant. She lays fifty million eggs a year.

Hulking Hercules

Hulking Hercules is a bulldog ant. She can lift more than twenty times her body weight.

The Big Biter

The Big Biter is a trap-jaw ant. She has the fastest bite in the animal world. Biter can snap her jaw shut at a speed of 145 miles an hour.

What's for Dinner?

Most ants catch and eat other insects.
Some ants eat dead animals.
Leafcutter ants grow their own food.
They have fungus gardens inside
their nest.

Leafcutter Ants and Fungus Garden

Q What did one leafcutter ant say to the other leafcutter ant?

A There's a fungus among us.

Aphid

WORD BITES

FUNGUS: A living thing that is not a plant or an animal. Mushrooms are a kind of fungus.

Many ants take care of aphids. Aphids are small insects. They make sugary poop that ants like to eat. Mmmm! Yummy!

How do you say aphid? Like this: A fid.

Army ants

Army ants hunt for food every day. The colony looks like a moving, munching carpet.

Army ants sting and bite everything in their path. They can kill insects, spiders, lizards, and baby birds.

An army ant colony can be as wide as a street. It can be longer than a football field.

Fire Ant

Army ants are not the only ants that sting and eat animals.

Fire ants have poison that they inject into other insects, animals, and even people. It leaves a burning feeling. That is how fire ants got their name.

There are more than 280 different kinds of fire ants.

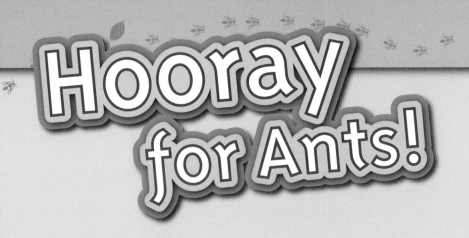

Hooray for Ants!

Ants are an important part of our world. They are food for other animals. Birds, frogs, and spiders eat ants. So do monkeys and aardvarks.

As ants dig tunnels, they mix the dirt. Plants grow better in dirt with ants.

Leafcutter ants dig up a lot of dirt when they build a nest. Scientists weighed the dirt one colony dug up. The dirt weighed as much as six elephants!

COLONY
A group of ants that lives together

FUNGUS
A living thing that is not a plant or an animal

LARVAE
The second stage in the life of many insects

PUPAE
The third stage in the life of many insects